A || P9-AGU-438

DATE DUE

			PRINTED IN U.S.A.

A SAMUEL FRENCH ACTING EDITION

SAMUEL FRENCH
FOUNDED 1830

SAMUELFRENCH.COM

ISBN 978-0-573-69153-9   Printed in U.S.A.   #3942

MUSIC USE NOTE

IMPORTANT BILLING AND CREDIT REQUIREMENTS

TABLE OF CONTENTS

Page

MAN AND WOMAN

TWO MEN

TWO WOMEN

MAN AND WOMAN

ROOMMATES

Drama. 1 man, 1 woman. Ages 16 and up.

AT RISE: JOHN walks into the living room and flops on the sofa next to ALAINA. It is past midnight. They are roommates.

JOHN. Whoa! What an evening! This night life is wearing me out!

ALAINA. Maybe you should try staying home once in a while.

JOHN. What and miss all the action?! I gotta keep up with what's happening.

ALAINA. The only thing that's happening is that you're turning into a zombie. John, you're burning the candle at both ends. Take a break.

JOHN. Since when have you been so concerned about me?

ALAINA. Since . . . (*Pause.*) Oh, never mind!

JOHN. Since what? Come on tell me.

ALAINA. It's nothing. Forget it.

JOHN. Hey, come on. We're buddies. Roomies. You can tell me. We share everything else, don't we?

ALAINA. (*Under her breath.*) Yeah. Everything except a bed.

JOHN. What did you say?

ALAINA. Nothing! I didn't say anything.

JOHN. Wait a minute. What's happening here? You've been giving me some really strange vibes lately. You wanna talk about it?

ALAINA. No!

JOHN. Well I do!

ALAINA. All right. I'm moving out!

JOHN. What? Why? What did I do?

ALAINA. It's what you didn't do.

JOHN. Would you tell me what's going on? We've been living together for two years. I've kept my end of the bargain. I didn't hit on you or sneak into your bedroom at night. I've been a good guy!

ALAINA. That's the point! I can't stand it anymore! You bring girls home all the time! I find underwear on the sofa, earrings in the bathroom . . .

JOHN. Hey, it sounds like you're jealous or something.

ALAINA. Well . . . maybe I am.

JOHN. Whoa. Does this mean what I think it means?

ALAINA. Just forget it! Forget it! I gotta leave.

(*JOHN grabs Alaina as SHE starts to leave.*)

JOHN. Alaina, would you stop acting so defensive? Let's talk about this. Maybe we can work something out.

ALAINA. It wasn't supposed to be like this. You were supposed to have your life and I was supposed to have mine. But somewhere along the way my life got tangled up with yours and now you are my life and I don't fit into yours. So I gotta leave. It hurts too much.

JOHN. Alaina! Do you know how many times I've wanted to take you in my arms, hold you, love you? But I didn't dare. I didn't want to jeopardize our friendship. I didn't think you wanted me. I went out so much because I didn't trust myself alone with you anymore.

ALAINA. (*Looking searchingly at him.*) Really? You really want me?

JOHN. Sweetheart, I've always wanted you.

(*THEY kiss.*)

FADEOUT

CATCH A THIEF

Drama. 1 man, 1 woman. Ages 16 and up.

AT RISE: FIONA is casually observing her guests. She lives in a magnificent mansion. The party is formal. A well dressed, sophisticated MAN approaches her from behind. HE shoves something into her back.

CAMERON. Don't turn around Fiona. Just smile and walk very slowly up the stairs.

FIONA. (*Loses composure for just a minute then does as she's told.*) Do you have a gun?

CAMERON. (*Smiling graciously.*) Oh, yes. Please do as I say. Now!

(THEY move into the other room. HE directly behind her.)

FIONA. I have this place electronically guarded. There are cameras everywhere. You won't get away with this. There are guard dogs out there that will rip you to shreds.

CAMERON. My dear Fiona, that has all been taken care of. You do look beautiful tonight. Is that Joy you're wearing?

FIONA. You want my body . . . is that it? Well . . . you'll never get away with it. I'll scream . . . I'll . . .

CAMERON. Please, my dear, don't worry. You can turn around if you like.

FIONA. (*Refuses to turn.*) Then you'll murder me because I've seen your face. I know the deal. I'm not going to look. Just take what you want and leave me alone.

(*CAMERON turns her around.*)

CAMERON. There! Was that so bad! I'm not a killer, just a thief.

FIONA. (*Looks at this good looking man with a little more warmth.*) Then why do you have a gun?

CAMERON. It's not a real gun. Just a water pistol. I don't need the real thing. Never had cause to use one. Now . . . all I want from you, Fiona, is the combination to your safe.

FIONA. Why should I give it to you? Who do you think you are, scaring me half to death? If you don't have a gun I'm leaving. I'm calling the guards! (*SHE moves towards the door.*)

CAMERON. I wouldn't do that if I were you.

FIONA. Why not?

CAMERON. There's a little matter about your taxes, Mrs. Vanderkeln. I do believe somewhere in the area of ten million unpaid dollars. The government would love to have the information and I can provide it. Would you prefer that? All that publicity? After all, I think there's probably only about five million worth of jewels in your safe. And definitely no jail sentence.

FIONA. How did you know about all this? Who are you?

CAMERON. Just call me Cameron.

FIONA. Cameron? Cameron who? How do I know you won't blackmail me again? How did you get invited here? Did one of my guests bring you? This is an outrage! This is blackmail!

CAMERON. One question at a time. First of all as a gentleman I shall give you my word that this little scenario will never be repeated. Secondly, all the information I have is in a post office box to which I shall give you the key. No, one of your guests did not invite me, and as for the blackmail . . . isn't that a little like the pot calling the kettle black? After all, tax evasion is right up there on the top of the list . . . so . . .

FIONA. How do you know I won't go to the police?

CAMERON. Because I think you like your freedom. Now enough chit chat. The combination. Let's make this easy. (*Pause.*) You're very beautiful, you know. The color in your gown sets off the sparks in your eyes or is that because you're angry at me?

FIONA. Are all thieves this charming?

CAMERON. I don't know. I don't think I know anyone else in my line of business. Perhaps a drink would ease the situation a little. What's your pleasure?

FIONA. You! You're my pleasure. What's the rush? Can you stay around a while? I mean after all, you're here . . . may as well enjoy yourself. My guests can do without me for a while and I have some champagne on ice in my bedroom . . .

CAMERON. Do you always keep chilled champagne available in your bedroom?

FIONA. Only when I'm expecting company.

(SHE moves in and THEY kiss.)

FADEOUT

HAIRDRESSERS

Comedy. 1 man, 1 woman. Ages 16 and up.

AT RISE: MAGGIE is sitting in front of the mirror in a hair salon. ALFREDO is her hairdresser.

MAGGIE. I don't know. I've never really had a different hair style before. I'm really nervous.

ALFREDO. Maggie, look at you. You look like a dog that's been caught in the rain!

MAGGIE. But I've always worn my hair this way! You never said anything about it before.

ALFREDO. Because I knew you weren't ready for a change. Now I can tell you are. How about going a little bit shorter on top . . . a little around the sides . . .

MAGGIE. How much shorter? You know I hear terrible stories about people getting scalped.

ALFREDO. Are you saying I don't know what I'm talking about?

MAGGIE. Of course not! I mean . . . well, my girlfriends have told me the time they just wanted a little change in style and have ended up with mohawks.

ALFREDO. (*Very indignant. HE walks around and sits in the chair next to her avoiding her look.*) Maggie, I refuse to touch your hair!

MAGGIE. Why?

ALFREDO. You seem to think I am one of those quicky jobs they do for $10.00 I happen to be the best in the business.

MAGGIE. Oh, I know that. I totally trust you, Alfredo. All I want is just a little change.

ALFREDO. A little change, eh? (*Sigh.*) All right. First I will change this dreadful color. It looks as though you fell in the mud.

MAGGIE. It does? But you recommended this color last time.

ALFREDO. Well, then it was in fashion. Now it's as old as Joan Collins. We need to lighten and brighten.

MAGGIE. Oh, I don't know. I just can't see myself as a blond.

ALFREDO. Who said anything about blond? I said lighten. Perhaps a little orange streak right about here.

MAGGIE. Orange?! Oh no! I couldn't do that! I work in a very conservative place. They'd fire me if I came to work like that. Oh no! Something less . . . well, less crazy.

ALFREDO. How do you expect me to work creatively if you don't let me follow my instincts?

MAGGIE. Alfredo . . . I don't mean to tell you what to do. I just want to tell you what not to do.

Perhaps you could give me a little trim around the bottom?

ALFREDO. A trim? Just a trim?! You call that a change? No, no you must trust me to do what I can to change you from the frumpy little person you are to a dramatic beauty.

MAGGIE. A dramatic beauty? You could do that?

ALFREDO. I can do anything. Just trust me.

MAGGIE. All right! I'll do it! I'll let you do whatever you think is necessary. Go for it, Alfredo! (*SHE closes her eyes tight.*)

ALFREDO. You won't be disappointed, Maggie. Here goes nothing! (*HE starts chopping off her hair.*)

BLACKOUT

MURDER IN THE DARK

Drama. 1 man, 1 woman. Ages 16 and up.

AT RISE: JESSIE is sleeping. An INTRUDER creeps into her room. HE walks over to her bed, watches her for awhile and then leans down to place his hand over her mouth. SHE wakes up and struggles.

INTRUDER. Shut up! Don't make a move or I'll kill you!

(SHE stares at him in absolute fear.)

INTRUDER. Do exactly as I tell you. I'm going to remove my hand from your mouth and you better not make a sound. You understand?!

(SHE is too scared to answer.)

INTRUDER. I said do you understand?!!!

(JESSIE nods her head.)

INTRUDER. Good girl. If you do as I say I won't have to hurt you.

JESSIE. Please don't hurt me. Please don't hurt me.

INTRUDER. I told you to shut up!

JESSIE. I'm sorry.

INTRUDER. You will be unless you shut up like I told you! You talk when I say you talk. Got it?

(*JESSIE nods.*)

INTRUDER. I want you to get up real slow, real slow.

JESSIE. What are you going to do? I have money in my dresser. Take it. Please. Take whatever you like.

INTRUDER. (*Leers at her.*) I intend to.

JESSIE. There's a family heirloom in the study. It must be worth about $100,000. Please take it and leave me alone.

INTRUDER. I know that, little Jessie. I know all about your family heirloom. But at the moment I'm much more interested in you.

JESSIE. Please. Don't hurt me . . . I . . . please . . .

(*HE touches her face stroking her hair and neck. HE moves in closer. SHE backs away. HE grabs her hair.*)

INTRUDER. Don't back away from me, little Jessie. You look scared. What do you think I'm going to do to you?

JESSIE. Please, please don't touch me.

INTRUDER. So you don't like me touching you, eh? Good! That makes it even more fun.

(*HE tries to kiss her. SHE pulls away running to the corner of the room.*)

INTRUDER. Come here, little Jessie. I want to make you real happy. You know it makes me real mad when you run away from me like that. (*HE pulls out a knife.*) Now, Jessie, do you know what happens to people who get me real mad?

(*JESSIE is shivering in fear. SHE is crouching in the corner.*)

INTRUDER. Come here! Come to me now! You little . . .

JESSIE. GET OUT! GET OUT!

(*SHE screams. HE walks towards her, the knife shining in his hand. HE grabs her by her nightdress collar and lifts her up slowly . HE puts the knife to her throat.*)

JESSIE. I'm sorry . . . I won't scream again . . . please . . . I won't run . . . anything . . . please,

please don't kill me. Please . . . no . . . NO . . .
NOOOO . . .

(*HE presses the knife against her stomach and with one swift movement stabs her. SHE falls to the ground while HE stands over her watching her die.*)

INTRUDER. I told you not to make me mad!
(*HE moves away smiling.*)

BLACKOUT

TENNIS, ANYONE?

Comedy. 1 man, 1 woman. Ages 16 and up.

AT RISE: RICK and DEBBIE are sitting around after a game of tennis.

DEBBIE. (*Pouting.*) Why aren't you talking to me?

RICK. I hate sore losers!

DEBBIE. Sore losers? Ha! I am not a sore loser!

RICK. Yeah, right! Is that why you stormed off the court after you threw the tennis racket at me?

DEBBIE. It slipped out of my hand.

RICK. It slipped all the way to the other side of the court?

DEBBIE. That's right!

RICK. Yeah, sure!

DEBBIE. If you hadn't of hit those balls so hard I could have returned them easily. But noooooo . . . . you had to use all your strength every time I scored a point.

RICK. What am I supposed to do? Do you want me to let you win?

DEBBIE. Of course not!

RICK. Well what do you want me to do? If I play hard you don't like it, if I let you win you don't like it! What do you want?

DEBBIE. I want a little more respect!

RICK. Respect? What has respect got to do with tennis?

DEBBIE. Everything . . . but of course someone like you wouldn't recognize respect if you sat on it!

RICK. How do you sit on respect?

DEBBIE. You know what I mean!

RICK. No! Enlighten me.

DEBBIE. O.K. . . . I think it shows disrespect if you yell, "she missed the ball! I can't believe she missed the easiest shot!" You embarrassed me in front of all those people!

RICK. Well, they could tell you weren't a very good player before I said that. What's the big deal?

DEBBIE. Not a very good player? Who do you think you are, Bjorn Borg?

RICK. Well let's face it, I'd give him a good run for his money.

DEBBIE. A good run for his money? Honey, you better wake up. You're a lousy player!

RICK. You're just jealous!

DEBBIE. Jealous?! Ha! You couldn't even beat my sister and she's only been playing six months!

RICK. YOU couldn't even beat your sister and YOU'VE been playing for six YEARS!

DEBBIE. So! You're a man!

RICK. You noticed!
DEBBIE. Barely!
RICK. Well in that case you'll barely notice I'm gone. Adios!

(*HE leaves. DEBBIE is left sitting alone.*)

DEBBIE. Men!

BLACKOUT

SPYING

Comedy. 1 man, 1 woman. Ages 20 and up.

AT RISE: MRS.SMITH is standing in her living room shakily explaining about a so-called prowler she claims she saw.

OFFICER. Mrs. Smith, calm down and tell me exactly what you saw.

MRS. SMITH. He was out there on my porch staring at me with binoculars!

OFFICER. All right. Did you get a good look at him?

MRS. SMITH. A darn good look!

OFFICER. Can you give me some details?

MRS. SMITH. Sure I can! He was so close I could've touched him if the window hadn't been closed. Scared me to death! Do you know what it's like to see a stranger staring at you so close?

OFFICER. Yes ma'm. Now could you describe what he looked like?

MRS. SMITH. You do know what it's like? Have you had someone do that to you? It's terrible, isn't it? I mean, one minute you think you're alone and the next . . . well I needn't tell you how frightening it is.

OFFICER. Ma'm, please give me descriptions on this person. We must have an idea of what we're looking for.

MRS. SMITH. He was tall . . . well he looked tall when he was crouching down.

OFFICER. How tall?

MRS. SMITH. Well . . . about as tall as Tom Cruise.

OFFICER. And how tall is that ma'm?

MRS. SMITH. Well I have no idea! How should I know?

OFFICER. 5'10" . . 6' . . . 6'4" . . . as tall as Magnum P.I.?

MRS. SMITH. Who's Magnum P.I.?

OFFICER. Mrs. Smith, was he tall or short?

MRS. SMITH. I told you.

OFFICER. What color hair?

MRS. SMITH. Brown . . . wait . . . maybe it was black . . . or was that a hat . . . ummm . . . I think it was dark brown.

OFFICER. So you think he might of had a hat on?

MRS. SMITH. It was dark . . .

OFFICER. O.K. Is there ANYTHING you can tell me about this intruder that I can use?

MRS. SMITH. Well, of course! He had a moustache!

OFFICER. Good, good. Anything else?

MRS. SMITH. . . . or what it a beard?

OFFICER. Ma'm, there's a big difference. If he was close enough to touch, surely you could tell the difference?

MRS. SMITH. Why are you getting mad at me? I'm trying to tell you and you're getting mad at me. I needn't tell you that I have a cousin on the police force that is a lieutenant!

OFFICER. So far, Mrs. Smith, the description could be anyone on this earth! Are you sure it was even a man?

MRS. SMITH. Does a woman wear a beard?

OFFICER. So it was a beard?

MRS. SMITH. Yes! It was a beard AND a moustache . . .well it was something on his face.

OFFICER. Could it have been a mask? A ski mask or . . .

MRS. SMITH. That's it! That's it! He wore a mask! That's why it was so frightening.

OFFICER. All right, Mrs. Smith. Thank you for your help. We'll do our best to catch this person.

MRS. SMITH. Thank you, officer. So glad I could be of such help to you. Let me know when you get him and I'll come and identify him for you.

OFFICER. . . . Ah . . . right . . . thank you, ma'm.

BLACKOUT

PICK UP

Comedy. 1 man, 1 woman. Ages 16 and up.

AT RISE: KELLY is sitting on the sofa of an open house. SHE is evaluating the rooms. SHAWN is wandering around and suddenly sees her. HE looks her up and down before casually walking over.

SHAWN. Nice house. Good price.
KELLY. Yeah!
SHAWN. Do you know it's supposed to be haunted?
KELLY. Haunted? Really?
SHAWN. Yup! About 10 years ago the old lady that lived here was murdered right here on the couch!
KELLY. (*Jumps up.*) Right here? On this couch?
SHAWN. Right here on this very couch.
KELLY. But the couch looks brand new!
SHAWN. Well . . . ah . . . yeah . . .they had it reupholstered. Yeah . . . it was a mess, I heard . . . blood everywhere. Terrible mess.

KELLY. My God, how awful. Is that why the price is so low?

SHAWN. Yeah! A lot of strange things happen here.

KELLY. Do they happen at night or during the day?

SHAWN. Both! Anytime the mood strikes.

KELLY. What happens?

SHAWN. Oh . . . you don't want to know.

KELLY. That bad? You know, come to think of it, it is very cold in here.

SHAWN. That's the first sign of massacred Maud!

KELLY. Massacred Maud? How did she die?

SHAWN. In bits and pieces.

KELLY. You mean . . .

SHAWN. Yep! The ax. Chopped off her head while she was peeling potatoes.

KELLY. Peeling potatoes . . . I thought you said she died on the couch?

SHAWN. Yeah . . . ah . . . well she was on the couch peeling potatoes . . . yeah!

KELLY. What?! Who peels potatoes on the couch? You're putting me on, aren't you?

SHAWN. Am I?

(*HE tosses his pencil to the far corner of the room. KELLY has turned away from him when SHE suddenly hears the noise.*)

KELLY. What was that?

SHAWN. Maud . . . it's massacred Maud. Over there! I say we get out of here and discuss this whole thing over a bottle of wine.

KELLY. I say that's a great idea.

(*Exeunt.*)

BLACKOUT

I GOT THE JOB!

Drama. 1 man, 1 woman. Ages 16 and up.

AT RISE: MICHAEL and RUTHIE are struggling actors, living together, loving together and supporting each other. MICHAEL comes running in and sweeps Ruthie off her feet.

MICHAEL. It got it!! I got the job!
RUTHIE. You got it?! You got the part?!
MICHAEL. I got the part! Can you believe it?! After all this time! I got the part!
RUTHIE. AHHHH . . . this is fantastic! When do you start? How much does it pay? Did they tell you how long you'll be shooting? Tell me . . .

MICHAEL. I start next week! Two grand a week and a three-year contract!
TINY. A three-year contract!! A THREE-YEAR CONTRACT?! Are you serious? They want you for three years?
MICHAEL. That's what they said! They love me! They're already putting together a whole publicity campaign. They're going to sell me to

the public before I even start the show. I can't
believe this. I gotta call my agent.

(*HE calls his agent while RUTHIE runs to the
kitchen and opens a bottle of wine. SHE
brings out two glasses full.*)

MICHAEL. Robert . . . Michael here . . . Yeah,
I just saw them . . . They called you? How about
that?! Yeah! . . . the whole works. What? You're
kidding, four grand a week after the first six
months? YEAH!!!

(*RUTHIE is in the background mouthing the
words "four grand". SHE pushes a glass into
Michael's hand. HE turns his back on her.*)

MICHAEL. Sure . . . seven tonight . . . La
Dome? Love it! Do you mind if Ruthie came?
(*Pause.*) Oh . . . o.k. . . . she'll understand.

(*RUTHIE looks hurt but tries not to show it.*)

MICHAEL. Hey, Rob . . . do you think they'll
have an apartment set up for me in New York?

(*RUTHIE turns quickly and gives him a strange
look. He hadn't told her the job was in New
York.*)

MICHAEL. Great! O.K. See you later. (*MICHAEL tries to ignore the look.*) Oh, man, Rob is so excited. We're going to celebrate at La Dome tonight. (*HE sees her look.*) Oh, honey. I'm sorry you can't come. It's just a lot of business and stuff to talk over. We can celebrate right now! (*HE reaches for her.*)

RUTHIE. (*Pulls away.*) Michael, what was this about New York?

MICHAEL. Well, there's something I didn't mention to you when I went for this interview. I guess I just figured I wouldn't get the job.

RUTHIE. (*Looks devastated.*) What? Michael please don't tell me you have to move to New York. Please!

MICHAEL. Ruthie, this is my career. Something I've been working on for years. The soap is filmed in New York. They want me to move there for three years. I'm sorry.

(*RUTHIE just stares at him.*)

MICHAEL. Please say something.

RUTHIE. I don't know what to say except congratulations.

MICHAEL. You can come with me. How about that?

RUTHIE. How about that? Yeah, how about that, Michael? How about the fact that I have a career too, or have you forgotten? How about the fact that we had planned to be married next year and settle in L.A. for good! How about all those things?

MICHAEL. That doesn't have to change. Wow, look at the time. I gotta meet Robert in an hour. I better start getting dressed.

RUTHIE. It's already changing! I can't even come to celebrate with you tonight! After all, who am I? A nobody! Certainly not the new boy wonder of soaps!

MICHAEL. Jesus, Ruthie! Give me a break! You knew this would happen to one of us someday. You knew that either one or both of us would make it. Don't begrudge me my chance. I would never do it to you.

RUTHIE. That's because you're the one that has the chance!

MICHAEL. That's not fair and you know it!

RUTHIE. Michael, I've lived in New York before. I hate it there. You know that! We always said we'd never live there. I wouldn't begrudge you if you had the job here. Our home is in L.A. All our contacts are here and I'm making headway in my career. I can't just walk out and start all over again in New York. I can't.

MICHAEL. and I can't walk out on this job!

(*There is a deep silence as EACH ONE feels the impossibility of the situation.*)

RUTHIE. (*Starts to cry.*) Then there's nowhere else to go with this conversation. It's a no win situation.

MICHAEL. (*Comes over and puts his arms around her.*) Oh, baby. I don't want it to be like this. But I would never forgive myself if I gave up this chance and you would never forgive yourself for making me. I love you. I want you with me.

RUTHIE. I would be miserable there. I'd make you miserable. (*Pause.*) Oh, Michael, what are we going to do?

MICHAEL. Right now you and I are going to celebrate! Come on, sweetheart, you're coming to La Dome with me. I love you. We'll talk about all this later.

RUTHIE. I thought Robert said I couldn't come.

MICHAEL. Hey, who's the star here? I said you're coming and Robert can think what he likes! I love you, baby. I always want you by my side.

FADE OUT

TWO MEN

RIVALS

Drama. 2 men. Ages 15 and up.

AT RISE: ALEX and GREG are staring each other down. ALEX is standing outside Greg's door.

ALEX. I told you if I caught you near Sherry again I'd beat your ass.

GREG. And I told you that if I wanted to see Sherry I would!

(ALEX grabs Greg's shirt.)

GREG. Get your filthy hands off my shirt! *(HE pushes Alex off.)*

ALEX. Man, you're gettin' me real mad! If I wasn't at your parent's house I'd beat the crap outta you.

GREG. Yeah, right! Just like at the parking lot, but that time there were too many people around! One excuse after another.

ALEX. If your father wasn't sitting in the other room . . .

GREG. . . . . you'd beat the crap outta me. Sounds familiar. Didn't you just say that? Do yourself a favor and get out of my house. You're giving the neighborhood a bad reputation.

ALEX. That's it, huh? You think you can do what the hell you like because you got bucks! You think you can just muscle in on my girl right under my nose?! Well pal, you can't! You wanna play big shot? Let's play in my neighborhood!

GREG. Listen, PAL, I don't have to prove anything to you!

ALEX. Just what I thought! Scared stiff to come over on the other side of the tracks. A real mama's boy. He's fine when mommy and daddy are standing behind him, but when it comes to some real fighting you're a total loser.

GREG. Right! And you call real fighting, a whole bunch of wigged out guys ready to finish the job if you don't!

ALEX. Hey, man, just you and me. Just you and me at Heller's Alley. Nine o'clock, tonight!

GREG. How can I be sure it's just you and me? The last time you called a dude out to Heller's alone he came home with twenty stitches and two broken legs! And there's no way you did that alone!

ALEX. That was different!

GREG. Yeah? How?

ALEX. He brought along a sawed off shot gun. Gonna blow my head off before I even saw him.

GREG. So if you were alone, how come your buddies broke him in two? You didn't know he had a shot gun.

ALEX. Man, you are so stupid! Nothin' gets past me, nothin'!

GREG. Not even the fact that Sherry can't stand you? That she thinks you're slime and that her parents won't even have you in the house or anywhere near it?

ALEX. (*Backs off in surprise.*) That ain't true, and you know it!

GREG. Hey, man, they say love is blind!

ALEX. I ain't blind and I ain't in love, O.K.!!

GREG. Right! Then why are you fighting with me if you're not in love with her?

ALEX. It's the principle of the thing, man! I told you not to do somethin' and you did it! That makes me mad! So ya gonna be there tonight or are ya gonna chicken out?

GREG. Hey, man, I got a better idea. Let's go to Kelsey's bar and get totally wasted and talk some more about this.

ALEX. On you?

GREG. Yeah. All you can drink on me!

ALEX. Deal! Let's go.

BLACKOUT

ACTORS!!

Comedy. 2 men. Ages 16 and up.

AT RISE: ANDY and the DIRECTOR are arguing over one of his lines. THEY are standing on the set.

DIRECTOR. Look, Andy. I need you to be a little more emotional when you read this line.

ANDY. But that's not the way I see it!

DIRECTOR. Well, that's the way it was written.

ANDY. Yeah, well it's too ordinary. Every actor could figure out how to read it that way. I wanted to get a different flavor into it.

DIRECTOR. Andy, this is a straightforward line! How many ways can you say "I love you?"

ANDY. How many ways can . . . how many ways can you say "I love you?" Thousands! Millions!

DIRECTOR. Not in this instance! Just say it like you mean it!

ANDY. I could shout it from the rooftops and mean it!

DIRECTOR. There are no rooftops in this scene!

ANDY. Well, let's build some!

DIRECTOR. Dammit, Andy! You're wasting precious time. Just say the line as though you mean it! GOT IT?!

ANDY. Yeah, I got it! But man, I can't work under this kind of pressure. I mean you yelling at me and all!

DIRECTOR. We have discussed this for over an hour now. There is nothing left to talk about . . . PLACES. (*HE walks away from Andy.*)

ANDY. (*Pouts off to a chair on the set.*) I can't do this scene now. You just took away the whole mood. How am I going to tell Jennifer that I love her with you yelling at me?

DIRECTOR. I AM NOT YELLING AT YOU!!

ANDY. Well if that's not yelling, I ain't talking at all!

DIRECTOR. PLACES!!

(*ANDY just sits there.*)

DIRECTOR. PLACES!!

(*ANDY still sits there.*)

DIRECTOR. That means you Andy!

ANDY. (*Gets up and paces.*) God! I'm so freaked out over this whole situation. How can I work under these conditions?!

DIRECTOR. Wanna try not working for the next three years?

ANDY. All right! All right! Resorting to threats to get a performance out of an actor. What next? FINE! I'll do it!

DIRECTOR. PLACES . . . LIGHTS . . . CAMERA . . . ACTION!

ANDY. (*Whispering.*) I love you.

DIRECTOR. CUT! What the heck was that? We couldn't even hear you!

ANDY. You said you didn't want it yelled from the rooftops!

DIRECTOR. I wanna hear it! Come on, Andy! Say it like you mean it, or is that too difficult?

ANDY. You mean like I said it in your dressing room the other night? (*HE makes a kissing noise towards the director.*)

DIRECTOR. That's enough! Do it now or I'll get someone to replace you. Got it?! No more games!!

ANDY. Got it, darling. I love you.

DIRECTOR. Wait for the camera! I want it just like that. O.K. For the camera. PLACES . . . LIGHTS . . . CAMERA . . . ACTION.

ANDY. (*Looks directly into the camera.*) I love you.

DIRECTOR. CUT! PRINT! That's a wrap! (*HE walks off shaking his head.*) ACTORS!!

BLACKOUT

MORTGAGE

Drama. 2 men. Ages 20 and up.

AT RISE: JOHN is sitting opposite MR. WITHERS, a banker. THEY are in deep discussion.

JOHN. There is no way I can make that payment.

MR. WITHERS. We've already extended your time by two months. This is as far as we can go.

JOHN. Look, I have this new job coming up. I'm trucking across to Canada. The money's great and I'll be able to make the full payment then.

MR. WITHERS. You told me that two months ago.

JOHN. Well, it just took longer coming than I thought. There was a big delay up North.

MR. WITHERS. What kind of delay?

JOHN. They had to wait for the snow to melt a little. The trucks couldn't get through to the mining camps.

MR. WITHERS. Well, I'm sorry but we just can't extend anymore.

JOHN. Tell my wife that, mister. We have four kids at home. I've been cleaning toilets . . . yeah toilets . . . for the past two months just to put food in their mouths.

MR. WITHERS. Look, I'm sorry you've had a rough time, John, but . . .

JOHN. That's MISTER SMITH . . .

MR. WITHERS. Look, MISTER SMITH, if I did this for everyone the bank would go bankrupt. You've no idea how many people come in with sob stories, begging for a little more time.

JOHN. And you just sit there giving them the same old story about how much the bank would suffer.

MR. WITHERS. There is nothing I can do. I'm sorry.

JOHN. So what does that mean? That I lose my house? That you can toss my family out into the streets? That I lose everything I've worked so hard for in the past twelve years? Just so your bank can keep a few extra bucks in the vault. For what? For what?!

MR. WITHERS. Mr. Smith, please! This is a bank. I would appreciate it if you kept your emotions to yourself!

JOHN. Of course you would. You don't want people to know what kind of person you are. Sitting there in your leather chair looking down at people that are less fortunate than you. Of course you want me to keep my voice down!

MR. WITHERS. Your outburst will serve no purpose, Mr. Smith. I suggest you apply for another loan, put up your truck for collateral. That will pay for the delinquent payments on your house.

JOHN. Is that how you got this job? Because you have no feelings? You know as well as I do that the only chance of getting work and getting there is by keeping my truck!

MR. WITHERS. I've given you all the advice I can at this time. There is nothing else I can do. Mr. Harbinger can help you with the loan application on the third floor. Now if you'll excuse me, I have other people waiting to see me.

JOHN. NO! I will not excuse you. You are a pathetic excuse for a human being. God help you, because one day when you really need a helping hand there isn't going to be one for you. People like you eventually get their just desserts. That's the way it works. I'll get your stinking money by tomorrow, Mr. Withers, but it won't be by selling my truck! (*Storms out.*)

BLACKOUT

NEIGHBORS

Comedy. 2 men. Ages 18 and up.

AT RISE: JEFF and BILL are facing each other at the door of Bill's house.

JEFF. I was hoping it wouldn't be necessary to come over here, Bill. But I gotta tell you that your dog has pooped on my porch one too many times. It's gotta stop.

BILL. (*Attempts to close the door.*) I don't have a dog.

JEFF. (*Puts his foot in the crack and pushes it open gently.*) What d'ya mean, you don't have a dog? You've had a dog for five years. All I'm asking is you keep him in your yard.

BILL. That dog you've seen for five years is not my dog, it's my wife's. You'll have to talk to her about it.

JEFF. Well . . . okay . . . is she in?

BILL. Nope.

JEFF. Will she be back soon?

BILL. I doubt it.

JEFF. In that case I'll talk to you about it and you can tell her.

BILL. Can't do that.

JEFF. Why not?

BILL. We ain't talkin'.

JEFF. This is ridiculous. Would you please keep your dog in your yard where he belongs? I can tell you it's no fun having to clean that stuff off your shoes day after day.

BILL. The dog goes where he pleases. I can't tell him not to poop on your porch. He don't understand English.

JEFF. Well, do you understand English, Mr. Bell? Because if I see that dirty mutt in my yard again I'm calling the pound!

BILL. Best thing you could do!

JEFF. What about your wife? I'm sure she would be upset.

BILL. My wife hates that dog.

JEFF. Then why have you had it so long?

BILL. Beats me.

JEFF. Look, I don't want to be the person that sends that dog to his death. Could you please be a good neighbor and keep him away from my house? I'm sure he's a great dog.

BILL. If he's such a great dog, why are you complainin'?

JEFF. Right! Right! If he's such a great dog why am I complaining? HOW WOULD YOU LIKE IT IF EVERY MORNING YOU CAME OUT TO GET THE MORNING PAPER AND STEPPED IN DOG DOODOO?

BILL. Well . . .

JEFF. Well . . . you'd be angry, too! You know it's not just my house he poops on, it's the other neighbors as well. Doesn't he ever do it on your porch?

BILL. Never! He only goes on other people's. Dogs never go on their owners' property. That's a well known fact, Mr. Jones!

JEFF. So you're not going to do anything about this?

BILL. Why should I? It don't bother me.

JEFF. Never goes on his owner's property huh? Great! (*HE leaves abruptly.*)

BILL. Where ya going? To get a pooper scooper?

JEFF. NO! TO GET A DOG!

BLACKOUT

JUST ONE

Drama. 2 men. Ages 16 and up.

AT RISE: MATTHEW and STEVEN are old buddies. Steven is trying to kick his alcoholism with Matthew's help. THEY are in Matthew's house. STEVEN looks a wreck.

STEVEN. Oh, man . . . I don't think I can do this!

MATTHEW. Stop thinking about it. Let's watch some T.V.

(THEY sit down and start to watch. STEVEN jumps up in disgust.)

STEVEN. Look at that! The first thing I see is a beer commercial. Please just turn the darn thing off!

MATTHEW. *(Turns it off.)* O.K. Let's play a game of cards.

STEVEN. The only way I can play cards is with a beer in one hand and peanuts in the other. How long has it been?

MATTHEW. Two days. Two whole days since you took your last drink.

STEVEN. Oh, man . . . my hands are shaking so bad. There's things biting my skin. Ow . . . ahh . . . they're all over my body. (*HE starts scratching himself, rubbing his skin in desperation.*) Help me . . . I can't stand this! I feel like I'm crawling with bugs. I'm going crazy!

MATTHEW. Splash some water on yourself.

STEVEN. Water? Water won't help! I need a drink! I really need a drink. Just one. I swear just one. Please. Please, Matt . . .

MATTHEW. Steven, come on man. You don't need a drink. Focus on your job, your girl, anything but booze. Remember what it's done to your life. Think how close you came to killing yourself with that stuff. It's poison, man, it's slowly eating away your insides.

STEVEN. I can't help it. I feel so bad. My whole body's on fire. I keep seeing things I know aren't there. I'm going crazy. I need a drink! Please, Matthew . . . just one . . . just a sip. Please. (*He suddenly jumps up and runs to the door.*) I gotta get outta here. I GOTTA GET OUT OF HERE!

MATTHEW. STEVE! The door is locked. I have the key. WE made a deal that I wouldn't let you leave this house in that condition. Come on, man, you don't need it!

STEVEN. HOW DO YOU KNOW WHAT I NEED? HUH? HOW DO YOU KNOW WHAT I'M GOING THROUGH? These noises in my head are driving me nuts! (*HE holds his head*

wandering off.) My head . . . it's going to burst . .
. Can't you stop this noise? (*HE starts to scratch
his body again.*) Ahhhhhh . . . this itching is
unbearable! Help me, man! Help me!

MATTHEW. Steve . . . I'm with you. It's
okay! This will pass. Just hang in, man, hang in.
You're doing great! Don't think of how much it
hurts, just know it will pass. Just talk to me about
your family, tell me what you're going to do after
this is all over. Talk to me, man.

STEVEN. Talk to you . . . talk . . . Okay.
When all . . . ow . . .when all this is over . . . I'm .
. . I'm . . .ahhh . . . my body's on fire, man.

MATTHEW. Keep talking. Focus on me.

STEVEN. When all this is over . . . ahhhh . . .
my skin! When all this is over, I'm going to take
my girl and get out of this city! I'm going to get a
new job . . . ahhhh . . . oh, man . . . this hurts so
bad . . . a new job, then I'm going to take a
vacation in the Bahamas. I'm going to do it! I will
not take another drink! I WILL NOT TAKE
ANOTHER DRINK! I CAN DO IT! I CAN DO
IT!! It's going . . . the itch is going! I can do it! I
CAN DO IT!!

MATTHEW. YEAH! YOU CAN DO IT!
MAN, YOU CAN DO IT!

(*FADE OUT with BOTH MEN shouting I CAN
DO IT!*)

CONFRONTATION

Drama. 2 men. Ages 17 and up.

AT RISE: MICHAEL and KIRK are staring each other down. The air is thick with tension.

MICHAEL. You really love her?

KIRK. Yes, I really love her.

MICHAEL. Does she love you?

KIRK. You'll have to talk to her about that.

MICHAEL. And what do you think she'll tell me?

KIRK. Why don't you ask her and find out?

MICHAEL. Hey, man! You're messing around with my wife and you stand there like . . . like . . .

KIRK. Like a man on a witness stand, while you give me the third degree. (*Pause.*) Look, Michael, I'm sorry. We never meant this to happen.

MICHAEL. You never meant it to happen? You mean you two have been sneaking around for the past twelve months and you never meant this to happen?

KIRK. What do you want me to say? Yes I knew she was married. She knew she was married. But it still happened! I love her! I can't help it!

MICHAEL. I love her too! She's my wife. Who do you think you are to come into my life and take the most precious person away from me? Who do you think you are?

KIRK. I'm the man who took your place when you were gone for months on end. I'm the person who comforted your wife when she got phone calls from all your girlfriends! I'm the one she began to trust, the one she laughed with and cried with. Man, you were never there when she needed you!

MICHAEL. I was never there when she needed ME? I needed HER out there on the road. I had no one to comfort me. She made the choice, man. She was the one who decided to stay home alone!

KIRK. Well, she changed her mind. She won't be sitting at home alone anymore. (*Gets his coat to leave.*)

MICHAEL. Hey, you better think again, Kirk old buddy. There is no way you're going to end up with my wife! GOT IT?!!

KIRK. Then you'd better tell her that!

MICHAEL. (*Moves in front of the door blocking Kirk.*) No! You better tell her that! You tell her that you two are through. I won't lose my wife to a two-bit guitar player like you. What can you give her? You got nothing! You live in a dump! You got no money, man! What do you have to give her? Huh?

KIRK. I got more than you'll ever have. To you the only thing in front of your eyes is dollar signs. Well, there's a lot more to life than money! Now get outta my way.

MICHAEL. You tell her that if she leaves me, she won't get a thing. Not one dime! I'll take the house, the cars everything! You got that, mister?! EVERYTHING!

KIRK. Yeah, I'll tell her. Good luck, man. I hope you'll be real happy with life. Now get outta my way . . . please.

MICHAEL. (*Moves from the door looking terribly sad.*) Tell her one thing for me.

KIRK. What's that?

MICHAEL. Tell her . . . tell her I love her.

(*KIRK nods and exits. MICHAEL wanders back into the house and sits down with his head in his hands and cries.*)

BLACKOUT

ON THE BEACH

Comedy. 2 men. Ages 15 and up.

AT RISE: JEFF and KIRK are sitting on the beach sunbathing while checking out the scene.

JEFF. Whoa! Check it out!

KIRK. Dude, what a ride.

JEFF. Narly surf.

KIRK. Dude, you could suffocate in those.

JEFF. Yeah, but what a way to go. Doin' what you like to do best.

KIRK. I'd like to just catch that wave and ride 'til I can't ride no more. Know what I mean, dude?

JEFF. Gotcha, dude. Seventh heaven.

KIRK. Oh man, I can't take this much longer. I gotta get some action.

JEFF. You?! Hey, I haven't seen this kind of action since last summer.

KIRK. Last summer? When you were in Hawaii?

JEFF. Yeah! Hawaii! Oh man, these ain't nothin' compared to those.

KIRK. Fifteen footers, huh?

JEFF. Easy. These are barely eight feet, dude.

KIRK. So you want to go and catch a few?

JEFF. Sure, dude. Are you ready?

KIRK. Yeah, I'm more than ready.

JEFF. Then let's go.

(*THEY pick up their boards when they see a gorgeous girl go by. BOTH stop in their tracks, mouths open, watching her as she walks away.*)

KIRK. What a babe! Dude, I could go for that.

JEFF. Man, you wouldn't have a chance.

KIRK. Wanna bet? (*HE takes off after her.*)

JEFF. Hey, what about the waves, dude?

KIRK. Oh, the waves. (*HE looks undecided, looking first at the ocean and then at the girl.*)

JEFF. She'll be here when we get back.

KIRK. A babe like that? Come one. Every guy on the beach is gonna make a move.

JEFF. Then you better make your move first, ole buddy.

KIRK. You think I'll have a chance?

JEFF. I think you'll have a better chance with the waves.

KIRK. O.K. the waves it is! Hey, maybe she'll see what a great surfer I am and come over to me. Yeah!

JEFF. Yeah, or maybe she'll see what a great surfer I am and come over to me! Yeah!

KIRK. Or maybe we'll both drown and never be heard from again.

KIRK and JEFF. YEAH! LET'S GO
SURFIN'.

BLACKOUT

TWO WOMEN

THE OTHER WOMAN

Drama. 2 women. 16 and up.

AT RISE: KATE is standing on the doorstep of Ashley's house. Ashley is her husband's mistress. ASHLEY ushers her in as SHE talks.

ASHLEY. Couldn't take it any longer, huh? Had to get a look at the other woman.

KATE. For your information, dear Ashley, I got a look at you a long time ago.

ASHLEY. Really! So why are you here?

KATE. To bring you some pictures I'm sure you'll be familiar with. (*SHE hands a tattered magazine to Ashley.*) It's open to a page.

ASHLEY. Where did you get this?

KATE. I have my sources, dear!

ASHLEY. This isn't me. (*SHE flings the magazine on the table.*) I would never pose nude!

KATE. Oh, really!? There's more in there. Photos that unmistakenly identify that birthmark on your ah . . . derriere. Unmistakable..

ASHLEY. What do you want?

KATE. What the hell do you think I want?

ASHLEY. Steven?

KATE. You seem to forget that I already have Steven. He is MY husband!

ASHLEY. Not for long.

KATE. (*Gives a little laugh.*) Dear Ashley, stop kidding yourself! Do you actually think he would want to be associated with an ex-hooker?

ASHLEY. I was not a hooker!

KATE. Whatever, but you might as well be when he gets a look at these pictures. No. You won't have Steven. He's worked too long and too hard over the years to have a little tart like you ruin his reputation. No, dear, you haven't got a chance.

ASHLEY. Steven loves me. He would understand that I needed the money back then. I was only nineteen. He would stand by me.

KATE. Then you obviously don't know him very well, do you? Steven is as ambitious as I am and nothing would get in his way to the Senate. You'd be a public embarrassment.

ASHLEY. Get out of my house!

KATE. Actually it's my house! That's another thing I came here to tell you. I want you out by noon tomorrow!

ASHLEY. (*Looks shocked and then quickly recovers.*) Oh, really! And just where do you propose I go? How about the newspapers? Shall I give them a little gossip of my own about dear Steven? About how he set me up in his own wife's house and used government spending money on his girlfriend's new Porshe? Or how about the time he had your jewelry stolen, and then collected the insurance money?

KATE. That's a lie! They're all lies!

ASHLEY. Are they, DEAR Kate? Do you have proof?

KATE. I don't need proof. You're a liar! The newspapers won't believe you. They'll laugh you right out of the newsroom.

ASHLEY. Not before I damage his career for good.

KATE. You little tramp!

ASHLEY. Takes one to know one!

KATE. I'll see you dead before I let you ruin my life. (*SHE storms out of the house.*)

ASHLEY. (*Turns away with a smile on her face.*) Not if I get you first.

BLACKOUT

THE RECORDING CONTRACT

Drama. 2 women. Ages 16 and up.

AT RISE: TESSA and LANE are sitting at a coffee table somewhere in Hollywood.

TESSA. Wow! Jack sure can play those drums. You don't know how happy I am to be with this band. We're going to be the hottest group this town has ever seen!

LANE. (*Far away in thought.*) Yeah. It's gonna be great.

TESSA. Earth to Lane. Are you still here?

LANE. What? Oh . . . yeah.

TESSA. Are you okay?

LANE. Yeah. I'm fine. It's just that . . . well . . .

TESSA. Well . . . well what?

LANE. Darn! This is so hard to tell you.

TESSA. (*Starts to get worried.*) Tell me? Listen if you've got something on your mind, let me know. Is it to do with the band?

LANE. Yeah. I just wish . . . oh darn! Listen, Tessa, there's no easy way to tell you this . . .

TESSA. What are you trying to say, Lane?

LANE. The guys don't want you in the band! There! I said it! Darn! I'm sorry, Tessa.

TESSA. They don't want me? But they picked me out of over a hundred girls. It took forever for you guys to decide. Why are you changing your minds? Why?

LANE. It's Mike's fault. He wants his new girlfriend to take your place.

TESSA. Just like that? (*Pause.*) Is she better than me?

LANE. I don't know. I haven't heard her yet. Mike says she used to play with Stevie Nicks and knows some pretty heavy hitters.

TESSA. I worked so hard to get this far! It isn't fair! Isn't there any way we could change his mind? I mean, after all, doesn't everyone in the band have to agree on this?

LANE. Well . . . I guess there should be some sort of vote.

TESSA. Would you vote for me?

LANE. Well . . . I suppose I should hear the other girl first.

TESSA. Yeah . . . right. (*Pause.*) What if she's really good?

LANE. Well . . .

TESSA. Yeah . . . right . . . what are friends for?!

LANE. Hey, Tessa. Don't take this so personally. We've gotta think of the band!

TESSA. And to heck with the members! I can't believe this is happening!

LANE. Listen, Tessa. I don't really know you that well but you have incredible talent and if you don't stay with our band there will be loads of others who would sign you on.

TESSA. Not as good as this one! Oh boy! I thought we were friends! I've been with you guys night and day for the last three months doing an album and now you say you don't know me very well! You want to just kick me out just like that?!

LANE. Hey, I'm sorry, O.K.! It's not my fault! They volunteered me to do the dirty work, that's all! I have to go now . . . are you coming?!

TESSA. With you?! You must be kidding! But you just give your precious band members a message from me. Tell them to remember my name because one day they're gonna be sorry they didn't keep me on. I'm the one that made your two bit band work! I'm the one that will make every top forty chart in the country and when you guys come sucking up to me I'll tell you all where to go!

BLACKOUT

SISTERS

Drama. 2 women. Age 18 and up.

AT RISE: CHRIS is sitting watching her sister. MELODY is devastated.

MELODY. How could you? How could you do this to me?

CHRIS. I didn't do anything to you. In fact I think I did you a favor.

MELODY. A favor? Is that what you call it? A favor? I just don't know what to say.

CHRIS. Then don't say anything. For God's sake, it's not the end of the world! We always shared everything else. What's so different about this?

MELODY. Jack is my husband! You can't just walk into my life and decide you want to sample my husband. I can't believe you could do this to me.

CHRIS. Honey, it wasn't only me that was doing the sampling.

MELODY. What?

CHRIS. Jack did his fair share of sampling his sister-in-law and, might I add, enjoyed every minute of it.

MELODY. I hate you! I hate everything about you. You're evil. You always were. You always lied your way out of everything. You stole from your own family and now this. You're despicable.

CHRIS. Oh, Melody. Don't get so uptight! You're so cute when you're angry but, honey, it's no good for the soul.

MELODY. Soul? What right do you have to talk about soul? Yours is obviously owned by the devil. You're hateful and cruel. Why couldn't you have gone after someone else's husband? Why Jack? Why?

CHRIS. I've had my share of everyone else's husband. It gets boring after a while. Same scenario. I needed a little spice. Besides, I always thought Jack was cute. And I think he always thought I was, too.

MELODY. That's enough! Don't you try to blame this on Jack. He loves me. He'd never do anything like this if you hadn't instigated it.

CHRIS. Let me tell you something, little Melody. Men are always available to a woman who knows what she wants and how to please him. In fact your sweet Jack went out of his way to let me know he was interested in a little rendezvous. So don't give me that innocent Jack routine. He's as guilty as me. If you can call it guilt.

MELODY. I don't believe you. Jack would never betray me like that.

CHRIS. Don't be so certain.

MELODY. I've never been more certain of anything in my life before.

CHRIS. (*Takes a sheet of paper out of her purse.*) Then you'd better have a look at this.

MELODY. What's this? (*SHE takes it.*)

CHRIS. Read it!

MELODY. (*Hands it back unread.*) NO! I don't want to read anything! Now just get out of my house.

CHRIS. Then I'll read it for you.

MELODY. NO! I said get out of my house!

CHRIS. "Dearest Chris, I can't wait to see you again. You bring excitement and danger to my life. I feel ten years younger. When can I see you again? It has to be soon. I'm getting buried under the pressures of marriage. Melody is so predictable and to tell you the truth . . . boring. We must . . ."

MELODY. (*Grabs the letter away from her sister and starts shouting over her sister's voice.*) STOP IT! STOP IT! I hate you! I despise you. (*Sobbing.*) Couldn't you have left me some shred of dignity? Did you have to read it to me? Did you have to?

BLACKOUT

DEPARTMENT STORE

Comedy. 2 women. Ages 16 and up.

AT RISE: KATHY is trying on different makeups in the department store. LIZ the sales girl butts in.

LIZ. That color would make you look like death warmed over.

KATHY. But this is the color I always use.

LIZ. See what I mean? You look so pale and washed out. What you need is to the Rose Nectar shade. So much more becoming on someone your age.

KATHY. I beg your pardon?

LIZ. Well, once you hit a certain age you need all the help you can get.

KATHY. For your information . . .

LIZ. Hold on a second . . . have you seen our latest shade of shadow?

KATHY. Yes . . . no . . . well actually I'm not interested in buying shadow today. I'm looking for a foundation.

LIZ. But you have such beautiful eyes. You should play them up a little more.

KATHY. Well, thank you. I usually don't bother with eye makeup during the day.

LIZ. Why? What's so different between night and day? I mean if you're going to be around people you may as well look your best.

KATHY. Well . . . I suppose you're right. I just never seem to have time to get all fixed up during the day.

LIZ. And it shows!

KATHY. What?!

LIZ. What I mean is . . . well . . . I see women come in here day in and day out looking like they just finished the laundry. They go out shopping with their hair in rollers, no makeup, baggy old sweats. I just think it's a shame that most women wait until a special occasion to look good. Don't you?

KATHY. (*Looks down at her baggy sweats, dirty sneakers.*) Well . . . since you put it like that. But the fact of the matter is that I was on my way to a workout and just dropped in to pick up one item. You caught me at my worst.

LIZ. And so did everyone else in the mall! Look I hope you don't think I'm being too forward by talking to you like this . . . it's just that I feel it's my job to help people become aware of their potential.

KATHY. I thought your job was to sell cosmetics!

LIZ. It is!

KATHY. Then why don't you stick to that! I think your customers would appreciate that more.

LIZ. Ohhh . . . we are touchy, aren't we?

KATHY. Lady, I've just about had it with you and your advice. For your information I happen to be the customer here and you happen to be the salesgirl. I make the demands here, you cater to them. You're nothing but a lowly employee behind a pretty counter. What you think doesn't matter to me. Now I want the Beige Melody foundation. That's right, the same as I'm wearing and the name of your superior.

LIZ. Miss . . .

KATHY. That's madam to you!

LIZ. Look, I'm sorry if I made you mad . . . I was just pointing out that women today . . .

KATHY. . . . are free to do as they please. So wrap up my makeup and keep your advice to yourself! That's a good little girl!

LIZ. Yes Ma'm.

BLACKOUT

SALE

Comedy. 2 women. Ages 16 and up.

AT RISE: BARBARA and GWEN are looking through a sale table. THEY both see the same item and grab for it.

BARBARA. Excuse me but I saw this first.
GWEN. No, I'm sorry, I believe I saw it first.
BARBARA. This is the only one of its kind. I saw it first.
GWEN. Miss, I had it in my hand before you even saw it!

(THEY are gently tugging at it.)

BARBARA. You most certainly did not.
GWEN. I most certainly did. Now give it to me!
BARBARA. Look, I've been everywhere trying to find a blouse like this. I'm sure you could find something else you like.

(BARBARA pulls it over to her side of the table. GWEN is still hanging on.)

GWEN. I happen to have been looking for a blouse identical to this, too. I wouldn't be happy with anything else. Now please give it to me.

(*SHE yanks it hard. BARBARA is still holding on as THEY have a tug of war.*)

BARBARA. NO! This is mine!
GWEN. It's mine!
BARBARA. Give it to me!
GWEN. I most certainly will not!
BARBARA. You most certainly will!

(*THEY tug at the blouse. Suddenly there is a loud RIPPING NOISE. THEY both drop it.*)

BARBARA. Now look at what you've done!
GWEN. What I've done?! Lady, you did it and I'm reporting you to the manager!
BARBARA. Oh, really?! And what are you going to say? That I stood here and ripped it in half?
GWEN. Exactly!
BARBARA. And you think she would believe you?
GWEN. Yes, I do.
BARBARA. You're more of a fool than you look. You are pathetic.
GWEN. How dare you!

BARBARA. How dare I? I dare because you just ripped up a blouse that I needed for tonight.

GWEN. Oh, now isn't that a shame. I think you should take it as it is. It couldn't look much worse than that rag you have on now.

BARBARA. For your information this cost $150.00.

GWEN. Yeah, I saw the same blouse in K-Mart. I think the price tag said $15.00!

BARBARA. Well, I should have known you shopped there. It shows!

GWEN. Not as much as that cheap wig you're wearing!

BARBARA. This is not a wig! This happens to be my own hair.

GWEN. On, my God! You're kidding! I wouldn't brag about it if I were you.

BARBARA. I've had enough of your vulgarity!

GWEN. And I've had enough of your whining.

(*THEY leave in opposite directions. Noses in the air.*)

BLACKOUT

THE HOSPITAL

Drama. 2 women or 1 woman, 1 man. Ages 18 and up.

AT RISE: The DOCTOR is sitting by DEBBIE's bedside in a hospital room.

DEBBIE. Come on, doc, you can't scare me!

DOCTOR. Debbie, the odds are you won't make it through surgery.

DEBBIE. Boy, you doctors never cease to amaze me! I mean you're so optimistic!

DOCTOR. What I mean is . . .

DEBBIE. Yeah, yeah. I know what you mean. You mean I'm havin' this operation for nothin'. Just so you guys can go to Bermuda for the summer.

DOCTOR. I understand what you must be going through.

DEBBIE. Do you? (*Pause.*) You really think you can sit there and tell me you know what I'm going through? You mean you can feel my pain, my fear, my heart beat so fast I sound like a runaway horse? HUH, DOC? HUH? CAN YOU

FEEL IT! (*SHE beats her chest sobbing.*) IN HERE?!

DOCTOR. Now, Debbie, calm down! It's all right. This operation may just change your life. There is a good chance you'll pull through.

DEBBIE. DON'T tell me to calm down! You doctors! YOU make me sick! You're so fake. You just don't get it, do you?

DEBBIE. Debbie! I want you to calm down. I'll have to give you a sedative if you don't.

DEBBIE. Sure! Pump me up with dope! You are so disgusting I wanna throw up. I hate you! I hate all of you! You can't make me better! You can't do anything!

DOCTOR. Debbie! Stop it! Calm down! Stop! (*Holds Debbie still.*)

DEBBIE. LET ME GO! (*SHE pulls away.*) Don't touch me! You have no idea how I feel! Don't pretend you do. I have thirty minutes before you shove a needle in my arm and send me off to a dreamland I may never wake up from . . . thirty minutes . . . twenty-nine . . .

DOCTOR. You will wake up and you will feel well. Don't do this to yourself. You're already telling yourself you may never wake up.

DEBBIE. Isn't that what you just told me?

DOCTOR. There is a 60/40 chance that you won't. But there is a forty percent chance you will pull through. It's up to you. The forty percent is attitude. That's what we need. The will to live.

DEBBIE. Suppose I got nothin' to live for?

DOCTOR. Debbie, you have the world at your feet. You're a famous recording artist. Everything anyone could possibly want. There're millions of people out there that are rooting for you. That love you. Come back for them.

DEBBIE. Come back for them? A lot of weirded out kids that live in a dreamland of their own?

DOCTOR. To them you are a symbol of hope. A person to whom they can relate. Kids look up to you. They admire your talents and your guts. Deep down they all want to be like you. Don't disappoint them.

DEBBIE. You really think so?

DOCTOR. That's the same speech my daughter gave me last night when I told her you faced surgery.

DEBBIE. She really said that? You mean it's not just hype? You think these kids really like ME?

DOCTOR. These kids really LOVE you.

DEBBIE. Love me? No one has loved me before. I mean loved me for me . . . you know.

DOCTOR. Well, if you look out the window I believe you'll see your entire fan club blocking the street. You won't disappoint them, will you? They're expecting a fifth album.

DEBBIE. (*Looks out window. SHE stares. SHE is moved.*) I won't disappoint them, doc. I won't disappoint them.

BLACKOUT

HANGOVER

Comedy. 2 women. Ages 15 and up.

AT RISE: LINDA and CANDICE are sitting on lounge chairs by a pool.

CANDICE. I feel awful. Why did I drink so much last night?

LINDA. I tried to tell you but you wouldn't listen. Just kept right on guzzling that champagne.

CANDICE. Ohhhh . . . my head is killing me. I must have made such a fool out of myself last night. I vaguely remember this gorgeous hunk helping me off the floor.

LINDA. Yeah, that was when you decided to see how many times you could spin around without falling over.

CANDICE. Did I do that? Oh, my God! I must have been plastered. Wasn't I soaking wet, too?

LINDA. Yeah! That was after you did a belly flop into the pool with all your clothes on.

CANDICE. Ohhhh . . . I can't believe I did that! I hope I don't see anyone I know today. I look ghastly . . . where's my soda water?

LINDA. You drank it all. Why don't you take a swim? It might help.

CANDICE. (*Starts to get up.*) Yeah, maybe you're right. (*SHE stops suddenly and sits down quickly, hiding her face.*) Oh, my gosh! Is it my imagination or is that the hunk from last night?

LINDA. Where?

CANDICE. Don't look! He'll see you! Oh, gosh, did you bring any lipstick with you?

LINDA. No I didn't, and how am I supposed to see if it's him if I can't look? (*SHE looks anyway.*) It is him! It looks like he's coming in this direction.

CANDICE. Oh no! Hide! Look the other way.

(*THE GIRLS are turning their faces towards each other in an effort to hide.*)

LINDA. For heaven's sake! He's bound to see us. It looks like we're trying to hide!

CANDICE. I just can't face him. I know I acted like a total idiot last night. I remember trying to serenade him. Ohhh . . . I don't know which is worse. The headache or the embarrassment.

LINDA. If it makes you feel any better, you were the life of the party! Everyone loved you!

CANDICE. Did Mr. Hunk like me or did he think I was just another drunk bimbo?

LINDA. Trust me, he liked you! Boy, did he like you!

CANDICE. What do you mean? Did I do anything bad?

LINDA. If you call stripping on the diving board bad, then yes, you did!

CANDICE. NO! I didn't! Did I?

LINDA. Nah! I'm only kidding. You were fine. Just loaded.

CANDICE. Hey, he's gone! The gorgeous hunk of man is gone. I may never know who he is. We may never cross paths again! I didn't even find out his name. Did you?

LINDA. Yup! Sure did.

CANDICE. Really? Who is he?

LINDA. His name is Christopher. He works as an editor on *Time* Magazine. He lives in New York City, comes to the coast all the time. Drives a red Mercedes 550SL convertible and has a gorgeous sister whose best friend got incredibly drunk last night!

CANDICE. Your brother! That hunk is your brother?! When can I see him again? Did you tell him I'm available? Is he still in town? We gotta go see him tonight. I can't believe he's your brother!

BLACKOUT